Martin Kämpchen

SIMPLY DO IT
DO IT SIMPLY

Martin Kämpchen

SIMPLY DO IT DO IT SIMPLY

Originally published under the title EINFACH TUN

Translated from German by
Matthew Pritchard

NIYOGI
BOOKS

Published by

NIYOGI BOOKS

D-78, Okhla Industrial Area, Phase-I
New Delhi-110 020, INDIA
Tel: 91-11-26816301, 49327000
Fax: 91-11-26810483, 26813830
email: niyogibooks@gmail.com
website: www.niyogibooks.com

Editor: Jyoti Kumari
Cover Design: Arati Devasher
Layout: Shashi Bhushan Prasad

ISBN: 978-93-81523-56-8

Publication: 2013

Printed at: Niyogi Offset Pvt. Ltd., New Delhi, India

Contents

I Waking

People in Europe live far from the equator, and are thereby at a disadvantage. In winter they wake up when it is still dark, and in summer when day has long since dawned. It is more natural to wake at daybreak, and to go to bed soon after darkness falls; in other words, to be woken by the first light of day and to be guided back to sleep by the gathering dusk.

The sun's course is like a great clock-face. When the sun appears on the horizon, the clock says: Awake! When it dips beneath the opposite horizon, the clock says: Sleep! For what is more natural and at the same time more wonderful than for us humans to imitate—better, to inwardly reproduce—the rhythm of the cosmos? Then the cosmos supports our life. In its stability it can provide us with a bulwark against the disorientating effects of catastrophes or crises.

The comfort that light enters the world and the sun rises just as we open our eyes—this can soothe much human suffering.

In India, religious people step outside, into the open after waking in order to greet the red dawn sun on the horizon. For them, the sun is the most powerful symbol of the divine that human beings can experience with their senses.

Enveloped by this strong, illuminating presence, we wake and fall asleep. This light shines on all our activities and accompanies each of our movements. We awaken from the darkness of sleep into this light and the light stays awake with us, strengthens our awareness, illumines our busy hands and enlightens our consciousness. For these reasons, the first feeling that we experience on waking should be a feeling of gratitude. We are grateful to wake again, to take part again in a day of creation. *Let there be light* says Genesis. We are grateful to feel newly created in this light.

With the first light we participate every morning in the new creation. Is there a happier way to begin the day?

Wishing peace upon others

When is the world more awake, more present, more itself than in the early morning? When is there such optimism vibrating in the air, as if we could wipe the past away like chalk marks on a blackboard and start anew once more? Only in the morning—very early in the morning. Sleep, if it is deep and prolonged, has the capacity to purify our feelings and thoughts. At the moment of waking we are in a state of weightlessness—we feel as if we are floating. We live in a fluid universe. Only gradually do we realise what tasks await us, and the day orders itself in our minds, with all its attractive and unpleasant activities. After that, we stand once more with our feet firmly planted on the ground.

The darkness of the night has the power to make colours, sounds, atmosphere and smells fresh again. In the early morning we experience nature as filled with renewed energy. But then we begin conversations, people run busily here and there, with hardly a thought for the world around them—and the freshness fades. The dust of the day settles on nature and on people. The world becomes heavy, and its weight presses down on us.

What can we do to keep the freshness of the morning in ourselves? We perceive the world and ourselves in a spirit of gratitude. Then we wish peace upon our fellows, upon nature and ourselves, every morning. We bless other people and nature, wishing them all peace.

We think of the people who are dearest to us, and say: *Peace be with you.*

We see the earth, the trees, the clouds and say: *Peace be with you.*

We think of all the people we will meet today and say to them: *Peace be with you.*

Through wishing peace, people and nature stay filled with energy. They remain true to themselves, remain pure and fresh. Through wishing peace we arm ourselves against unpleasant surprises and depressing experiences. To be at peace means to be at one with oneself, to be in equilibrium, to stay pure and filled with the power to act. When we pass the day with the thought of peace present in our minds, nothing can truly disturb us. And as soon as our own peace is threatened we find support in the peace of humanity and of nature.

Trusting

We must start practicing trust. We consider it modern to exercise suspicion, to pick holes, to see most things in a cynical light. Skepticism and mistrust come easier to us than having trust in people and their ideals. It is easier for us to universalise our own disappointments than those positive experiences where people and their ideals have achieved success. Complaints get a more sympathetic hearing than accolades. What a pity that we often have to force ourselves to be happy at the happiness of others.

If we are incapable of trust, then we are depriving ourselves of one of life's most elemental experiences. Trust in life—in the fact that we are alive and will carry on living—was the fundamental attitude of our childhood. Then everything seemed life-affirming, our needs were always accommodated. We could eat and drink whenever we wanted. We were petted and carried around without earning it through any achievement. This unconditional love affected us deeply. It gave us that original trust that life is worth living. This trust is the deepest kind of pleasure in life. It unites us with creation.

How did we lose this trust when we became adults?

The enemy of trust is fear. I do not mean healthy, respectful fear of a higher being, but irrational, panicked fear of the unnamable. It squeezes the energy of life out of us. This fear exudes skepticism and mistrust, flooding us with pessimistic emotions. It whispers to us that the basis of our life is not an original trust, but a primeval fear.

We can only combat this fear by practicing trust in life. We must reassure ourselves daily that creation exists: the sun rises, clouds pass across the sky, the river flows toward the sea, a tree stands firmly planted in the earth, the wind rustles its leaves, people stroll along the road—creation is! And we are in the middle of creation. We breathe within it, we move within it, we sleep and wake at its centre.

Breathing

At one point in history, a feather would be held under the nose of a dying man for confirmation. If it moved, it meant he was still breathing; and if he was breathing, he was alive. Breathing is a life-sustaining activity. A practiced observer may even be able to recognise from our breathing how we live; whether we are quiet or excited, joyful or depressed, anxious or high-spirited. Our breathing is short or shallow, deep or jerky, the breath circles down to the bottom of our lungs, or is already reflected from the chest back up to the mouth and nose.

The worrisome thing is that we are seldom aware of our breathing. We do not perceive that we breathe, or how we breathe. Our senses are directed outward. We see and hear, are overjoyed or sad—and we think that these are the essentials of life. But our breathing is more essential. If you have ever been unable to breathe, you will know the truth of that. Breathing is the most elementary freedom that we human beings enjoy. Just because breathing is so fundamental, it points to the creator who—according to Genesis—breathed the breath of life into the first man, so that he became a living soul. For that reason the first thing we should be aware of in the morning after we get up is our breath. *I breathe therefore I live!* We are filled with gratitude that we draw breath and live: gratitude towards life and towards Him who created it. Breathing in and breathing out, in continuous, equal rhythm, accompanies us throughout the day. All rhythms follow the same cycle: from activity to rest, from receiving to giving, from opening to retracting. The life of the cosmos is a continuous transformation, night to day, winter to summer, wilting to flowering. Through our breath our own life is linked in to this rhythm. Breathing in moves us to draw up our energies, to recover, to eat modestly, to pray, to meditate, to contemplate, to play and listen to music. Breathing out gives us the courage to intervene in the world, to dedicate ourselves to others, to build on our life's work, to struggle for peace and justice, to prepare ourselves for suffering.

When we consciously take part in life through the rhythm of our breathing, and thereby take the measure of both our outer and our inner life, then we observe in amazement that we are able to breathe more deeply and regularly. As we do so our moods and thoughts become more restrained and proportionate; for they too are shaped by our breath.

11 Striding out

Making strides is a practiced and conscious mode of walking. Must we practice putting one foot in front of the other? We did that as children, surely we have long since put it behind us! Only pay attention to how a model walks down the catwalk or an actor across the stage: like athletes, who achieve the peak performance through their limbs' carefully calculated arcs of movement. Actors do not aim at athletic perfection but at charismatic effect. They express something with a precise, minimal use of the resources at their disposal. Charisma is the ability to project outwardly an idea or an energy that inhabits one's mind, one's heart or one's body, immediately and in one sweep. A person's potential is clearly and powerfully reflected in their external appearance, which has an effect on other people and on their environment.

A charismatic stride expresses self-awareness, pride, enthusiasm, a sense of beauty, and spiritedness. The higher emotions, in other words, those which develop independently of life's entanglements, of our social surroundings or in spite of them. A practiced stride is a celebration of one's moral and intellectual independence. One's head is held up, looking straight out.

He who makes strides does not labour.

He who makes strides sees and watches over far horizons.

Those who measure their strides also measure their energies. They know that they do not crawl, but neither do they fly. In striding out they are neither fleeing something, nor do they fear being overtaken.

A woman in Berlin once showed me her unusually large living room. She said, 'I must be able to stride up and down in my flat'. For her, that was the epitome of living in style. To stride out means that we take possession of the open spaces around us that we use and enjoy them. To measure our strides is a special way of enjoying the open space and freedom that others saunter, rush or march past heedlessly. With such striding out I take gentle but definite possession of the world; but then I must give it back, because for me, the freedom of space is just as precious as my own freedom.

Climbing steps

Flights of steps in a city should be approached for the first time always from the bottom, and ascended. Climbing up from step to step we observe an ever wider circle of our surroundings. The horizon expands, we rise above the people on the road, above the cars, above the trees, the electric pylons, the street lamps, and finally we see clear across the roofs of the buildings. People throng in the streets far below, we can make out their heads perhaps, their bodies hardly at all. In the end we cannot even see heads, but only groups of dark points that wait together at the side of the road or cross it in sudden spurts; we see cars moving almost soundlessly, driving alongside or behind other cars, stopping and starting according to some mysterious, spectral set of laws.

A single will appears to determine the rules of these movements. We feel a harmony in the various movements of so many points—as if the whole city, with its people, cars, streets and houses, were one body.

There we stand high up at the top of the steps, looking down, and feeling ourselves to be at a great distance from everything. With our mind unencumbered, we see how people on the flat land below us, race around, pause, start off again. They believe that every detail they attend to has a purpose. Up here, however, we see no details, only the whole.

We look down as if upon our own life. We become calm. It does us good.

Then we climb down again, listening and watching step by step the changes that occur. What an experience, to descend again into the roar of the streets, among the houses and trees, among the cars and the people. Our gaze descends even to the withered leaf on the roadside. We will never again let our sense of tranquility be overpowered by such commotion.

I love heights, but closeness is just as precious. I love the gaze from afar, but I also need the touch of people, their breath, and the sparkle in their eyes.

Wandering

In everyday life we stride out towards fixed destinations. We walk only in order to be able to do something else afterwards. In this way we have little profit from walking itself. But when we say, 'I'll go for a wander,' we step out from pure joy in movement. In wandering we return to being human. We are not teachers or businessmen, labourers or engineers, neither are we like those who drive cars or watch television. No motor propels us forward, no windscreen divides us from our surroundings.

In wandering we experience nature and people in their own innate rhythm. If we drive past in a car we might see two geese in front of a farmer's house, but we cannot observe how they waddle from the house to the garden, how they cackle and stretch their necks, how they march one behind another phlegmatically. From the car we see only snapshots. But as wanderers we experience whole processes and relationships, we experience complexes and paradoxes. Snapshots are hardly mysterious, but relationships always are.

When we wander, we feel no obligation to do anything else that might meaningfully fill up the time. To wander along, performing always the same, rhythmical and mechanical walking movements is enough. These movements satisfy our impulse to activity, but they do not occupy our heads. As we wander our heads remain free—free to observe, to take in, to delight in the forms of nature. Those who later forget what they have seen have nothing to reproach themselves with.

One's head is free, but one's feet sense the firmness of the earth beneath them at every step, declaring their own solidarity with the ground. Only these continuous movements in even tempo make wandering, with its freedom and experiences, possible.

Wandering is only fulfilling if one gives time to it. No one would call walking for an hour wandering. It must be several hours, several hours without interruption! Only then do we feel as though we really were absorbed into the life around us. We are neither guests nor spectators. Increasing physical fatigue is accompanied by an extraordinary transparency of the spirit, as if—like in a dream—it wanted to free itself from the body.

Opening doors

A closed door is like a dark wall—an open door promises distant, manifold horizons. The closed door makes our imagination stray—the open door lets it fan out, flutter off, to touch, hear, and see, to smell and taste, divining behind every sensuous experience other, ever new ones. The horizon may be ever so far off, but there must still be something behind it which the senses cannot reach, something remaining to be discovered. Is it not marvelous that the earth is round? Only in this way can horizons always conceal something from us. Even from the furthest viewpoint—say, from the moon—one can still only see half of the earth.

To open a door is only the beginning of a journey, not the satisfaction of our longing. The further we travel, flinging open door after door, more feelings of dissatisfaction can work their way into our minds. We become that much more willing to submit to imagination in order to fill out what we have experienced. But our imagination always needs a supply of fuel if it is to be set ablaze. It burns, and constantly seeks that which can be burnt. It wants to change its horizons, or at least to recall opened doors and the surprises that lay behind them. Patience and self-sufficiency are foreign to it. To be sure, when the imagination burns too furiously, then it sets us on fire and threatens to suffocate us. Then, aghast, we seek to shut ourselves away in calm and safety.

We live our lives in an inescapable and essential alternating movement between the registering of impressions and flights into our own imagination. The scales never stand still in perfect balance, but rise and fall constantly. We need both: the door opened, but also closed. If it is shut, we want to open it; if it stands open, then after a while we are overpowered and want to close it again. Again and again we seek out the protection of a closed, narrowly limited space which will filter out the harshness of the outside world. But we are no foetuses in the womb now; soon we feel suffocated in our caves, and push our way out. At the start of every journey I feel impelled by a fate-like force driving me forward. I cannot do anything else, I must go further forward, always forward. After some hours, however, I understand again what I must accept—that my fate is one thing I must shape myself. We are summoned to freedom from the moment of our birth. Again and again we must struggle to translate this knowledge into action within everyday life, trying to keep the scales in balance.

Packing a suitcase

What do we take with us when we travel away? Someone travelling by car has it easy: the car boot has lots of space, the difficulty of decision-making is only moderate. But if we travel by train, if we have to change trains and carry our suitcase by hand over long distances? Our knees threaten to buckle, half-way up the flight of stairs we are out of breath, we are confronted with the fearful prospect of fighting through the crowds in order to climb into the train. Then we have to reflect: what do I really need? Not this, and not that! In reality we need little, and are startled at the fact. A load is taken off our minds.

On the one hand, we perceive the many things that surround us in the rooms of our house as pleasant and calming, and we would not be separated from them. On the other hand, they turn into a burden when we become suddenly, uneasily conscious of how few of them actually give us pleasure. Many objects are lifeless, lying or hanging there because they were always in that spot and we left them there for convenience's sake. If we were to rearrange our surroundings every year, creating a new atmosphere for our lives, they would become more vital.

It refreshes us if we practice certain asceticism, sparsity and clearing of our living space, only gathering around us what we could pack into a suitcase. This sparsity makes us attentive, we use things more consciously. We notice, astonished, how enjoyable it is not to have to choose, but to be reliant on the little that is there. We take care that objects of daily use function, and are not misplaced. With purpose and love we build up around us a world of vital, meaningful things, and recognise more clearly that we are the centre of this little cosmos. We forget nothing; every object retains its immediate connection with us.

That we can live with such few things, as few as they fit into a suitcase—even if it is only for a short holiday—takes on significance. Then we take firmer control of our circumstances; we become freed from the service of so many things and so many people. This lends us an inner freedom which was scarcely imaginable before. Loss of the ability to choose, limitations of this sort may seem to us at first like a reduction in our quality of life until we notice that we lack nothing. Then inner spaces open themselves to us. Not to have to choose signifies a gain of energy and time for what is more essential. A person who lives out of a suitcase gains an unsuspected new outlook on the world.

III Greeting

When two people meet, they look for an appropriate signal of recognition and appreciation. They shake hands, they embrace, kiss each other on the cheek, hail each other loudly with arms raised, or silently with folded palms. Most forms of greetings permit people to touch one another. How closely, for how long, or how emphatically often expresses how well they know each other and how much they yearned to meet once more. The more contact there is, the clearer it is that their greeting is no longer just a symbol of pleasure and affection, but already an experience of encounter and an expression of relationship.

Indians greet each other with palms pressed together in front of their chest. They stand opposite one another and give a little bow, their hands folded. Do they not touch, then? Indeed they do, for the contact of their gazes is already 'touching'. A ray passes between the eyes which, like an electric current or a magnetic attraction, connects the two like light. This creates the moment of touch. There is recognition in this touch, just as when the apostles recognised Jesus Christ after the Resurrection when his gaze met theirs.

The Japanese bow to one another a number of times, palms on thighs. This simultaneous bowing is performed to show mutual inclination and respect. It is not touching, but rather an invitation to harmonious co-existence.

How tender is an embrace with kisses on the right and left cheek. The lips are drawn momentarily together and open with a tiny puff into the air. The warmth of the embrace is only suggested, and this airy fleetingness is more charming and radiates more than many a formally executed gesture. Nevertheless it can be just as seriously meant.

A handshake can never be merely suggested. It cannot be cut short; it must be forceful and decisive. There is thus nothing airy or charming about it. For a moment it turns two people into each others' prisoner. It is not surprising that it dates from the epoch of chivalry. The pressure of the hand enforces duties; through it one can make agreements binding, but a handshake will never be the gesture of loving welcome.

Offering praise

To praise is harder than to criticise. Finding fault with people comes easily to us. We need only take a couple of steps to the side, wait half an hour, or sense the slightest disruption in our mood, and what was irreproachable before now seems dubious. A slick haircut suddenly seems vain, an ironed shirt self-important, a beautiful song kitschy, an exciting story over-long. To criticise small details can feel like a sign of sincerity: in doing so, one shows that one has dedicated sufficient time and attention to the other.

Yet if one always only criticises, and finds fault with everything, then in the end one is no longer taken seriously.

On the other hand, words of praise can easily sound superficial, like an excuse, if we cannot substantiate them thoroughly. Such praise is not encouraging, but disappointing.

If, however, we possess a basic attitude which is prompt to recognise and praise others, we will be listened to with respect. This fundamental attitude shows itself in our listening and watching with concentration and concern, in the way we ask questions and await answers. In our recognition and declaration of the good, the vitalising aspects in any situation. In our willingness to particularise, to explain why we liked this but not that. This sort of differentiated praise is confident and genuine. It does not only specify objectively, but is mindful of the situation of the person to whom praise is offered. How can we nurture them and lead them forward? How can we even free them from a false opinion of themselves through selective praise? Differentiated praise always contains criticism too, through what we do not dwell on or leave out of our commendations. In all of this we should nonetheless never be too sure of our own judgment. Perhaps we ourselves are under the spell of illusions and a false sense of self-worth.

Praise only has substance when it makes visible the value of life and of creation. In and from this flows the praise which one person offers to another. And so it should be given accurately, using speech and silence together with care.

A word of praise can last a lifetime; a missed chance to praise can inhibit one for just as long.

Asking questions

If we are unwilling to listen attentively when our questions are answered, we should not ask questions to begin with. Those who introduce questions into their monologues merely as a passing inflection, or who use the other's meek reply as a way of asserting their conversational dominance, are the sort of people better avoided. We ask questions because we are curious about the answers. We ask in the right way when we create an atmosphere in which answers can unfold themselves naturally. We listen to our interlocutor's reply all the way through. Then we react to it; we do not continue our own line of thought as if it made no difference.

I have had the experience of conversations in which the other person would talk and talk and only at the end, out of politeness, not out of real interest, say, 'Now you say something!' To that there is no appropriate response. On the one side, after such a verbal onslaught a single question is quite insufficient to restore balance. And then, it is humiliating to talk only after having been given 'permission' to do so. One becomes the other person's excuse for not having to feel guilty of outright filibustering. The guilt is however not something I am inclined to relieve him of. If someone says to me, at the end of his monologue, 'I am glad we had such a good conversation', then I will avoid him in future. I would rather not be imposed upon.

Questions and answers are easily subjected to the dynamics of power. The more powerful partner in the conversation dominates it thoughtlessly, and the other stands obediently and listens, for in the end he needs the goodwill of the one with power.

There are exceptions, of course. When people want to communicate deep suffering or inner distress, and can relieve their feelings through talking. Or when elderly people feel overpowered by memories or fears. Then simple listening and timely questions are the intelligent response.

Questions and answers are a human affair, and in this sense just as important as the ideas and information that they are used to exchange. In conversation we should not only see and hear the other, but sense them constantly as a personal presence. We conduct conversations in order to communicate. Thereby we appreciate what things we have in common, we sense the 'chemistry', tune into the 'wavelength' of the other person. The discovery through conversation of things held in common often makes us happier than a growth in our knowledge or opinions. For that we always have books and newspapers. Knowledge that we have gained through the discovery of shared experience acquires a deeper meaning; it becomes engraved in us.

Arguing

I find people suspicious who live together and never allow themselves to come into conflict. Either they avoid any sort of conflict by remaining silent in the face of alternative opinions, or they have such a superficial and unfocussed way of living that it offers no grip for someone who might attack it. Everything is alright by them. But if one wants to shape one's life consciously, one must daily remind oneself: *I want to do this and not that, I want to have this and not that.* So conflicts within me and with other people are unavoidable. One trait of a strong and candid character is not to circumvent these conflicts but to accept the tensions and frictions that come with them. Even personal animosities and the damage they may cause to one's career are inescapable. The only way out would be to repress our convictions, out of cowardice.

Arguing does not mean getting heated about something, or telling the neighbour who threw a loud party last night what you think of them. Arguing means struggling to know the truth. Arguments are thus only sensible in the absence of strong emotions. The strongest positive feelings and the strongest negative feelings cloud our judgement in like manner. For this reason polemics never have long-term consequences. They may bring about changes in the current state of affairs, but they never bring about a change of heart. We do not happily allow ourselves to be pushed into a corner and then publicly corrected—that counts as an injury.

For a few years now people have talked of a 'culture of argument'. Arguing becomes a cultural project if the partners in the argument can muster the tact to bring the other closer to the truth, without causing them personal offence or humiliation. That presupposes that the opponents in the argument esteem and appreciate one another, and are arguing for the sake of the topic.

It is essential to a culture of argument that we do not immediately blurt out everything we think; that we leave out for the time being the less important elements of our disagreement for the sake of a peaceful result; that we recognise on what point and at what moment the other person might be capable of changing their mind. A culture of argument must recognise the beauty of compromise. It prizes the satisfaction that we gain when our views converge, be that ever so slowly or partially. But a culture of argument also knows the moment at which one must withdraw from an argument, because it cannot lead to a result. Even in argument we must spare one another's feelings.

Embracing

When two people who love one another meet, they fall into each other's arms. This close contact of bodies expresses how strongly the separation was felt, how much they have longed to be together. Eye-contact is not enough then, nor any facial expression, nor taking the other's hands in yours. Complete separation can only be cancelled out by the closest proximity, by the greatest possible bodily contact.

Each person flings their arms around the other, pressing their body against the other. For a moment they rest like this in the other's arms, feel the other's body and their own body in relationship to the other, and then they release each other again.

In this brief moment something astonishing occurs. Both feel a sense of commonality, of coming together as one, even of true oneness. How can contact of such short duration stir us like this? A stirring which reaches the other, is recognised and responded to, and is reflected back to the first person?

In this example we are made aware of the power of touch, which within the shortest time span can either connect people or injure them.

When two people embrace, they are both defenseless. They allow their freedom of movement to be restricted by the other, they voluntarily give themselves to one another. An embrace is a declaration of peace, bare-handed and helpless. We yield ourselves with empty hands to the other's embrace, offering each other this gesture of trust.

Therefore it is the very nadir of treachery and abuse if an embrace is used to expose someone's weaknesses—as when Judas delivered Jesus into the hands of his enemies. Or when someone is embraced and then stabbed in the back—as Caesar was by Brutus. Then everything which the embrace signifies is transformed into its opposite.

Keeping silence

Speech is not silver and silence is not gold. Gold is instead the right amount of speech and silence. When the situation demands that we speak, we should not keep silent. Every situation requires its own exact weighing of words and silences. To sense out the true measure of these demands of us a fine awareness, breaking through every cliché, every prejudice and every habit.

To keep one's mouth shut is childishly simple by comparison. Should we have decided to keep silent in a given situation, however, it is not enough simply not to speak. We must know exactly why to keep silent. Either there is nothing to add, because everything necessary has already been said by others. Or we ourselves are at the end of our knowledge and would at best be repeating ourselves.

When we are silent, our feelings and thoughts should also cease, settle themselves. It would be dishonest to oneself to run in circles inwardly, whether in exultation or indignation, and keep one's lips pressed together the entire time. Silence opens a space of contentment and leisure within us that we should look on affirmatively and seek to protect.

The custodian of silence is our sense of proportion. 'Rejoice with them that do rejoice, and weep with them that weep', says St Paul. Joy and sorrow have their entitlements in our lives. But let us be careful of emotions that may bubble over—negative and positive. Neither rejoicing to the skies nor sorrowing to death are fitting reactions to reality. Sooner or later an emotional backlash will follow that puts both rejoicing and sorrow in question.

Consider that feelings and thoughts are the origin of our words and actions. Somehow, sometime, what moves within us will find its way to our lips and to our hands. What is important therefore is that our feelings and thoughts are restrained, so that our words and deeds can also remain so.

The space of silence within us must be so consolidated that words and silences weigh and order themselves organically within it before emerging. Only then does silence avoid being a capitulation to what is spoken by others, or to their greater knowledge. Only then does it become a force as strong as words and deeds. And only then is speech not the destruction of silence but its fulfillment, just as silence can fulfill speech.

Travelling by train

Is it not a wonderful thing, to sit and do nothing but gaze out while the train takes us through the countryside? The train determines the route, travels slower or faster, stops and moves on, lets people on and off—all this is taken care of for us, whilst we look out of the window and observe things passing by, until finally it is time for us too to get off. It is not surprising that we fall to musing, philosophising. As we glide through cities and along the banks of rivers, long-ago worlds form again within us. Our memories reach far back into the past; next to what was, we set what could have or should have been. The serenity of these idle hours is shot through with brooding thoughts.

Meanwhile, in the train a kind of domestic life is unfolding—in public. People hold conversations, they read, talk loudly on the phone, stretch out, doze or sleep soundly, sometimes snoring. A few hack doggedly away at their laptops. Many behave as if they were alone; some, however, open up to the people around them and seek out contact and conversation. Or they arrive with their friends or family, and continue in the compartment the discussions they had been having on the platform.

Whether they got on alone or in a group, the travelers become a community. They are after all sitting in the same carriage and travelling in the same direction. All of them have a destination, where they want to reach on time—perhaps some of them have somebody waiting. The sense of community becomes evident when something unusual occurs: a lengthy stoppage between stations, an accident, the rude behaviour of a fellow-traveler, a sudden rerouting. Then everyone starts a discussion with everyone else, as if they already knew each other; there arises a sense of common fate, and each person wants to be sure of their neighbour in order to overcome their own insecurity. Him over there—he knows what's going on! This man will advise us! Out of an anonymous community a living and functioning one is created. The train carriage becomes a microcosm. This human variety was always there, only no-one wanted to perceive it—the point was to get to where one is going! Now the words and the body language of each traveler tell their own story. None of their lives is anonymous—they become individuals. When the disturbance passes and the train carries on, then the quiet life of the train, animated by its own gently musing atmosphere, returns once more.

IV Remembering

The past is one of man's most important treasures. From it we draw our inspiration, our maturity, our decisions and also our fears and negative feelings. It is essential for us to bring our past into our present through memory. This is the conscious endeavour to make the past fruitful for our present life. That occurs when we do not reject and repress it, but instead shape our lives (the more lovingly, the older we are) out of the experiences it contains.

When we row in a boat across a lake, we look at the smooth surface of the water and feel how the boat glides across. How much more mysterious does the journey become, though, when we imagine the depth of the lake, when we perhaps sound its bottom and then become conscious that we are floating on ten or twenty meters of water. The journey of our present is like this: it leads us over an ever-deepening space, that of our past.

Our memory has the happy attribute of making a selection out of the images, sounds, smells and stories of our past—a positive selection. Even experiences which were negative and regrettable when experienced singly appear for the most part bearable, or less aggressive and threatening, in the endless web of memory. It is possible, and easier the longer ago they occurred, to take something good away from our sad, dismaying or disappointing experiences. At least we can say, 'Good that it's over'. At least we know which experiences to avoid.

The optimism our memory encourages can catch up to the present and become a general optimism about life, if we acknowledge our past and do not deny or trivialise anything. For the past cannot be destroyed. It remains, even if we cannot comprehend the last remainder of it with our senses, even if we forget so many events, so many details.

If one wants to attain mastery over one's life, one should learn to live equally in the past and the present. Our never-ending task is that of keeping both in harmony. When past and present flow together, moments of timeless presence arise. It is in these moments that true happiness is concealed.

Standing

The flower stands on a stem so thin that one fears it will snap. But it does not, and the flower remains upright; just as we do. Our feet are, in comparison with our bodies, so short and narrow that one is surprised how they can support the body's whole length. We associate with standing ideas such as stability and fixity. In reality, standing needs a continuous balancing of our weight, which we shift from one foot to the other. True stability only exists in lying down, when the maximum amount of surface contact with the ground can be obtained; a position that can therefore be kept without moving for a long time. But lying down we associate with rest, sleep, laziness—not with stability.

Standing is a form of asceticism. The continuous balancing of our weight demands presence of mind. Monks stand for hours at a stretch during communal prayers. Standing expresses their preparedness to receive god's call. The early Christian stylites who stood on pillars took this asceticism to an extreme. Day and night, in wind and in rain they stood alone and unprotected on a pillar.

Standing reveals itself as an attitude of mind, as soon as we recognise the connection between our unsteady balancing and the solid earth on which we stand. Our wavering and tottering expresses our quest for stability. In seeking support we want to be like the solid earth. In standing we want to give our body—and with it, our thoughts and feelings—that stability which we feel beneath us. The earth should grow up in us and imbue us with its stability.

In earlier times people used to read and write while standing. We know the tall writing desks in the monasteries and the lecterns in the churches. The alertness that the writing and reading of sacred words demanded was expressed, and at the same time promoted, by the scribe's or the reader's physical posture. Compare with that our contorted crouching at the computer, our half-sitting-half-lying to read on the sofa, and we come to realise that true mental engagement demands a corresponding posture and movement from our bodies.

Flying

Even after so many decades of travelling long distances, I still have a feeling of adventure every time I get into an airplane. In wonder, I experience how it starts from the runway, accelerates, races at top speed across the ground, lifts off, and climbs and climbs.

Human beings cannot fly, they have no wings. When they manage it with the aid of technology, it seems like a miracle. Technology gives people the ability to make themselves light, as light as the wind. The air and the winds are invisible, their lightness hardly manifests itself. But the flying man—look, there he glides, between the clouds...

When our bodies are lightened, lifting the laws of nature, then the forces of inertia within us should lift too. The consciousness of flying, this sensation of wonder and astonishment, awakens a feeling of intoxication in us. Our mind looses its moorings and begins to float. It throws its ballast overboard and moves off by itself.

Consider the seductiveness of flight: normally we must make an effort to reach any height above the earth. We climb steps, or a mountain. We have to struggle for that view from the heights. Our gaze takes in everything up to the furthest horizon, and yet our feet remain solidly planted on the ground. But not when we fly. There we are marvelously, effortlessly borne aloft. Beneath us, above us, everywhere there is space, open space, wonderful open space! Our habitual feeling of space is superseded.

The intoxication of so much freedom can be dangerous. Keep control of your mind in its flight; do not abandon it completely to weightlessness!

When we fly, our familiar sense of time also disappears. Time as divided into hours, minutes and seconds only seems to count when our feet are on the ground. As soon as we are lifted up and begin to fly, time stops its mechanical course—it starts to daydream, to float, to soar. On long flights, such a blurring of time's movement intensifies into a feeling of unreality. The feeling of time's progression from one day to the next drops away, our memory of what happened yesterday or the day before grows hazy. Flying is still one of man's dreams.

Crying

Crying and laughing are not speech or silence. They are a third category, created from our sudden inability to formulate a sentence combined with a desire to react in some form. Crying and laughing are forms of speechlessness (and I would consider calculated silence one of the tools of speech). Something was said, something has happened that brings us up short or strikes us down so powerfully that we 'lose our tongue'. But what we have just experienced is so strong, so unusual that we are compelled to react. We are at the mercy of a powerful reflex that we cannot control. Then we begin to cry or to laugh.

We laugh with our mouths and cry with our eyes. But that is not really true: the whole face is what weeps, it is distorted into an unrecognisable mask, which disconcerts or dismays or even disgusts other people with its ugliness. People who cry isolate themselves. One can only cry for oneself and in answer to one's own pain. Crying can be infectious, but it does not create a deeper feeling of community. Others become silent and sad when they see us weeping, but they feel embarrassment in front of our tears. We experience crying as a painful self-exposure. Everyone struggles to bring the feelings which have been shattered into chaos back into order.

Crying is a kind of violence to oneself. Emotions break out and express themselves violently, heedlessly. But this violence is sometimes, for brief periods, necessary, so that we can heal ourselves. Tears cannot be repressed, and we should not try to repress them. That would be an unhealthy, contrary act of violence. Our powerful feelings could not relieve themselves then, they would tear us apart inside. Long-brewing resentments or emotions such as anger or grief would flare up uncontrollably and continue to put strain on us.

But we should not voluntarily allow any more space to tears than they seem to need. Weeping should not spread out like a fire. Crying exhausts us physically and emotionally. The best comfort is a good, long sleep.

Then we should recompose ourselves and return to our familiar face, the one cherished by others. The pain and grief may not be over yet. But we can talk about them, reflect on them and find different symbols and gestures for them, in order to thread them back into the texture of our life. Tears by themselves do not heal us. We must heal ourselves from them.

Fearing

Fear of god counts as a virtue, but not fear of other people. That is condemned as cowardliness, anxiousness, weakness. But I see fear of other people as a concession to reality. Fear of others acknowledges that not all people are equal, that some are stronger or more powerful, cunning, or merciless. At the bottom, everyone has a reason to fear, for even the powerful have someone above them. Those who boast that they fear no one are living in a topsy-turvy dreamworld.

In India, not only children but adults also admit, without hesitation, 'I am afraid'. That is a sufficient explanation for why one does or omits to do something. In general, no one tries to argue other people out of their fear. The acknowledgement of hierarchy is a practice with which children are already acquainted. It preserves them from excess and extremes and from the denial of reality.

Fear ought not to be blind or irrational. On the contrary, it should teach us to keep our eyes open, and take the exact measure of people and the things of this world. Fear is the admission that one has nothing in common with certain people, and that one should keep one's distance from them. Our resistance towards people who inspire fear and our orientation towards people who evoke sympathy—these are the scales that hold our life in balance. Someone who fears nothing will also give no space to sympathy, to inner resonance with others. Fear and sympathy condition one another.

Fear of other people, when this is fear of something more powerful than oneself, points to fear of god, the most powerful being of all. We should encounter him with awe, with holy dread, with 'fear and trembling'.

The goddesses of Hinduism frequently display two kinds of *mudra* or symbolic hand-gesture: one means *Take my blessing*, the other, *Do not fear.* When Jesus appeared to his disciples after the resurrection, the first thing he said was, *Do not fear.* That means that god wants to relieve us of our fear. Those who look upon god, who see his fearsomely shining, world-shaking true face and overcome their fear, they are relieved of all fear, including the fear of other people. They need not watch the scales of fear and sympathy, for they know that god places trust and love above fear. Those who trust in god cannot fear any more.

Concentrating

Imagination and concentration are locked in perpetual battle. The world belongs to them who can unfold their imagination, and also, but in a different way, to those who can concentrate. People who live in ever new imaginative spaces, deriving one from the next, are like nets: the wider they are spread, the more they catch. Concentrated people are like arrows, which reach targets further off, the slimmer and sharper they are.

Living in a world of multiplying images means being able to rejoice at their abundance, to enjoy through them the world's riches, to experience in them sadness and happiness, ecstasy and bitterness. But to use this world of images for a solid achievement, for works and deeds, it must be subdued, focussed, put into a structure and perspective, so that out of it something is created which communicates with other people, and produces certain feelings and thoughts in them. We must concentrate in order to create such a work. The more we can prolong our concentration, the more ambitious and demanding that work can be, the more closely it will shape our inner world. People who are overpowered by images and plans that they have dreamt up, but cannot project these outwardly, remain captives of their fantasies. Those who only have a talent for concentration but possess no ideas, images or stories of their own, no 'material' that their concentration can shape—their lives are barren, and their ability likewise can scarcely bear fruit.

Distraction is the enemy of anyone who wants to build a life's work. Distraction is like a sieve through which all good thoughts, impressions and intentions drain. For it is not enough merely to have good ideas and interesting feelings, what matters is that we can also express them and make them into a shaping power in our lives.

People who always feel disturbed in their concentration, who are always waiting for that happy moment of full composure, will never find it—their lives will be wasted. We should be content with the degree of perfection that we can achieve with our resources, our will and determination. The work that grows from concentration is always a product of a gritty battle for concentration itself.

When we bring imagination and concentration into a balance in which the material of our imagination is tamed by our power of concentration—then we can bring forth a remarkable life's work.

V Lighting a candle

We sit down at a restaurant table, and the waiter lights a candle for us. We visit a church, see innumerable little flames in front of a statue or an icon, and add one more candle, lit from one of those already burning. We may even like to have a candle on the table in our apartment.

Why? In poor countries, people light lamps or candles when the power goes off in the evenings. Then the flickering little flame must light up the whole room. By its glow children study, men work, women cook. By contrast, in Europe the flame is not there to break the darkness but to warm the space emotionally, to make it more convivial or festive. The flame is a modest but valuable luxury, not an article of daily use.

What makes the flame something special? It lives. It radiates light and warmth; it moves, flickers, flows, jumps and trembles. It seeks sustenance and air. The lighted candle on the table gives us the feeling that we are not alone. As living beings we compare ourselves to the living flame, and feel it gives us company. We seek company more than anything else—and find it in light.

The company of people is unreliable. Some say, 'I will come' but they never turn up. Others say, 'I will stay' but they soon leave. The flame, by contrast, is faithful. As long as it has sustenance, the wax, the tallow, the air, it stays constant.

But do not touch! Otherwise the flame will consume us. As Jesus said after the resurrection, 'Touch me not'. He was like the sun, which we cannot touch, cannot even look at directly. And the flame too has something transfigured, something unapproachable about it. It holds faith with us from a small but insuperable distance—that is its mystery.

Sitting

Someone who sits does not intend to move about, but also has no desire to rest. Sitting is the posture of mental effort. Someone who sits is seeking that comfortable physical stability which allows one to forget one's body in order to concentrate on intellectual activity.

A yogi cements such stability by sitting cross-legged, so that not only the feet and posterior touch the ground, but also the thighs, forming a V shape. This way of sitting is unshakeable, imperturbable. Since a person's physical posture and mental attitude influence one another, outer imperturbability will transmit itself to one's inner state.

In essence, every kind of inner activity calls for its own physical posture or physical movement. Even sitting is not simply sitting. Someone writing will bend forward; someone reading will lean back. Someone thinking rests their head on their hand. Someone meditating will sit with a straight, erect back, their chest pushed out. Someone listening will tilt their head forward almost imperceptibly in order to catch the other's words. Someone speaking will try to sit freely, without relying on any support.

When sitting, one's arms and legs are adjusted to find that posture relative to the central axis which will sustain one's mental processes. Of course one's centre must not be unbalanced, and freedom of movement has its limits. One's arms and legs create and maintain equilibrium, reconcile centre and periphery, inner and outer spheres.

When sitting, we are conscious that we can work uninterrupted. When sitting we can bestow, administer, control. We possess authority. We do not serve, neither do we love; rather we prepare everything, try to understand, lean back and listen, ask questions, plan, and make decisions.

Whilst we are sitting we scarcely sense the passage of time. Time waits for us to stand up, for our dynamism to be kindled, for us to deliver the plans we have accumulated and matured.

Praying

Someone praying does not make conversation, they do not speak, they do not listen. Praying is so different from everyday activities that they cannot paraphrase it. When we pray, we close off our senses: we do not see, we do not hear, we do not taste. We direct our words to the unknown, something that can neither be understood with the senses, nor grasped in our hands. Nevertheless, we speak words of adoration, of trust, of love, and surrender our secrets and our desires to this unknown being. Seen in a matter-of-fact way, how senseless that appears! And yet how steeped in sense and significance our behaviour appears to us.

Prayer is the assertion of meaning in the face of doubt, indifference and cynicism. Praying gives no answer to the question of why it is meaningful; it simply occurs. Prayer is naked, inscrutable being. Why is a rose red? Why does a tulip bloom in the frosts before spring comes? What is sleep? These are similar questions without answers. But they are also questions that need no answers. An answer would neither explain the beauty of the rose, nor be able to produce it. Someone who prays understands what prayer is and what effect it has on us. Someone who sleeps understands what sleep is and what effect it has. To understand prayer and sleep, one should experience them.

It may be that we are ridiculed or looked on as strange when the fruits of prayer become manifest. Prayer creates its own world in us—and around us. Only we who pray are allowed inside. There we are alone, but in a fulfilled way. We pray, we adore, we wonder, and do this alone—and that is enough. We do not try to reach a goal or a result—nothing of that sort. And yet this suffices. We cannot compel a rose to flower, nor determine when we fall asleep.

One result can be named: the unknown, the great 'Something' is there, if we can only sweep everyday life out of our senses—and pray. The words that we choose may seem banal, but they come from the depths of prayer. And so they are like magic words, creating a world in which we are face to face with something that we no longer need to name.

Waiting

Scarcely anyone tolerates waiting easily. It is always introduced by some irregularity: the train is delayed, the guest does not arrive on time, there is a traffic jam on the road. How such interruptions in the course of our daily life incense us! We are wasting time, we think. Waiting is empty time, it is the opposite of fulfillment. We have set goals for ourselves, and dates and times have been fixed. Everyone demands that we keep to them.

Waiting means having to make haste later on, dangerously accelerating the rhythm of life, taking on the harm that may result in order to catch up with ourselves.

Those who experience waiting like to believe that they are masters of time. They hold to the naive belief that they can shape time unconditionally—as long as such interruptions do not arise. Is there anything more foolish? This 'as long as' shows the fragility of their attitude. One thoughtless step, and they stumble and fall. One hasty movement, and they strike their head against the wall. One restless night and they get up with pains in their chest. It only takes a draught for them to feel a cold coming on; a bad dream for the morning to start off on the wrong foot; a spiteful word for their blood pressure to rise.

The counterpart of waiting is haste. Those who wait impatiently are overpowered by time. Those who make haste want to overpower time. Both disrespect time's sovereignty. People who hurry want time's net to hold more than it can; but time will have its revenge, its net will burst and all sorts of unsuspected, unconscious things will spill out. People who wait are themselves caught wriggling in time's net, and feel the danger of falling out.

Time is our capital. If we deal with it like an independent business partner, we can use this capital. Every minute of waiting that is—on the face of it—empty can be usefully filled with reading, prayer, reflection, a moment of ease, of meditation, or of relaxation. An interruption in our activities is not an interruption in time. Let us fill it further with experience. It is only the suction, the dragnet of time's flow that we must escape.

Haste is just the same: we should never sacrifice the rhythm of our life in the belief that we can outwit time. To slip ourselves back into time's order is something we must practice.

Lying down

If one is lying down, it is easy to stay there. By contrast with standing, sitting and kneeling, lying is a physical posture that we can maintain for hours without movement. We lay down after we were born, and before we die we will do the same. We are lying down in moments of greatest pleasure and of most terrible pain—and when we sleep, when we are released from both pleasure and pain.

Lying down is the basic posture of physical yoga, from which all its exercises begin and to which they return. Lying down is the basic posture in a second sense: in lying down we have the most contact with the basis of all our postures, the earth. We are formed from this earth and will return to it. The seriousness of this is best brought home to us when we lie down upon the earth, for in this position we feel ourselves nearest to the earthly element in us.

This contact with the earth from the shoulders to the buttocks, from the back of the head to the heels, and with hands, arms and legs, is healing; the solid and unchangeable nature of the earth beneath us feels like a supporting power. Lying down means drawing energy, which we then apply to activity as we stand, walk or sit. In lying down, the body is relaxed because it feels secure on the solid earth. For another few minutes the nerves and muscles twitch. Then they calm themselves too, and we are flooded with a feeling of well-being.

In lying down our feelings and thoughts also attain rest. Our will is no longer tensed. We forget the passions that have driven us; they subside like water flowing down and gathering at the deepest point. Sometimes old fears surface that we fight against by standing up, and engaging in an activity of some sort. But we are more likely to begin dreaming, become sleepy and sluggish and feel it as a gift not to have to move, either physically or mentally.

Lying down is truly a gift, and we can receive it so easily. Therefore we should make conscious use of it: we should prefer a flat, hard bed, so that we feel the base on which we rest. To begin with it may seem uncomfortable, but after a few days the hard surface becomes our friend. In a mysterious fashion the hardness of one thing pressing on another disappears, and we no longer feel the difference between our body and what supports it. Then we have truly received lying down as a present. Then lying down soothes every violent movement of the spirit and gives energy to our exhausted body.

Swimming

Why swim, when we can walk, march or run? Walking is man's natural means of locomotion. Walking upright is what distinguishes human beings. Swimming is for ducks and fish, flying for birds and bees. Fish will never learn to walk and bees will never learn to swim. Ducks swim and waddle, birds fly and hop about—they command two realms at least. But no one commands all three. Only we human beings constantly strive to be at home in water, on the earth and in the air. If Nature sets limits, then technology will extend them. We fly with airplanes and dive with oxygen cylinders.

And yet swimming for us humans is truly neither fish nor fowl. We will never achieve the mastery of it that fish and ducks possess. Our arms and legs are no replacements for fins and webbed feet. Our attempts at swimming are paltry and inelegant. After a few minutes under water we are desperate for air. Is that what tempts us to swim? To be able to boast: 'I can swim like a fish!'? To feel a pleasure that is not truly due us? Just because water is not our element, we savour it with all the more relish. To swim through the water—this taste of freedom...the delight there is in those few moments in the world beneath the surface.

Glider pilots, parachutists or snorkelers are dependent on their equipment. Swimming is an elemental joy, for we need only our body. The water touches our whole body, we feel it more immediately than the invisible, almost imperceptible air that surrounds us on land.

In the water we experience a spontaneous unity of our body and the element that surrounds it. Suddenly we are no longer just a body, we are far more powerful than we ever experience being on earth. We transcend our native, human limits and feel a great enthusiasm in being one with the water, something fish perhaps never feel. They live in their element and are content with simply being fish. Human beings however enrich their sense of being human when they dive into the water.

VI Drawing water

In Indian villages there still exist old-fashioned wells, with a metal bucket pulled up and let down on the end of a length of rope. The bucket hits the water at the bottom, it dips under and is filled. Then it is drawn up again on the pulley. Hands tug on the rope alternately until the bucket appears at the edge of the well. What an adventure, to fetch water thus out of the bowels of the earth!

Far below at the bottom of the well shaft, barely visible—there the water lies, like hidden treasure. Even though it seems to have been there for an age, when it is drawn up to the light of day it still tastes fresh. Does the darkness of the earth keep the water so vital? Does it stay like that because no gaze can reach it, no hands can touch it? Is it the peace in which the water rests, down there, which makes it so appetising?

From every stratum of the earth, water drips and trickles down into the well. An inexhaustible reservoir, renewed from mysterious sources. Is the earth, then, not really as solid as it feels to us on the surface? Deep within there are constant movements; water drips and trickles into the permeable ground, the earth concedes little spaces in which water collects, the soil slips, shifts, creates tiny channels and tiny barriers. Earth and water are secretly in motion, interacting, working, pressing, giving way to or withstanding pressure. And we draw from the depths water that has been filtered and purified by the earth.

Water pumps spare us manual labour, but they also deny us the pleasure of communicating with the earth in this manner. Fountains which, thanks to technical refinements, can spew water through metal spouts and mouths into bowls or basins lose this mystery. They are meeting-points, focus-points, they bubble and spray great spouts of water, and in cities they provide at least a point of contrast with the traffic. But they only fill the air, and hardly point into the depths out of which they draw their meaning.

Drinking

Man shall not live by bread alone, says the gospel. He lives just as much by the food of the spirit. Yet we know that we would waste away if we did not also drink. People need water, we are told, and we are given calculations of how many litres per day are necessary. But do we drink water? We drink carbonated mineral water, lemonade, cola, tea, coffee, beer, juice and wine. But often we do not like tap water; it is said to be unhealthy. Even if it is perfectly safe we spurn it—it 'doesn't taste of anything'.

Say we have been exerting ourselves, we have been sweating. Our mouth contracts from lack of moisture. Our tongue becomes heavy. We want to swallow but have no saliva in our mouth. Suddenly we are prepared to drink even tap water, and at the first gulp we feel refreshed. It feels quite different from the satiety caused by eating bread. When bread is chewed thoroughly it is dispersed within our body. After a while we feel the gain in energy, feel rescued from the strange limpness and uneasiness of mild hunger. Sated, we become a little lethargic and sleepy.

While drinking, however, we experience even as the liquid runs through our body, a joy and lightness, an inner mobility, a kind of floating—feelings that are different from the satiety produced by solid food. There is no heaviness or feeling of indigestion. Water breathes life into us directly. This water, which flows everywhere in streams and rivers, which is stored up in lakes many miles across, and which flows into our taps virtually free of charge—just water is the one which fills us with life, which is so precious, so delectable, which lengthens our lives and imbues us with a feeling of elation. Since it 'does not taste of anything' it contains every taste, sweet and bitter. Since it is present in abundance and easily accessible, it is nature's most universal, all-embracing gift.

Eating

Eating and drinking keep body and soul together, we say. Certainly, eating gives strength to the body which burns energy every minute. Our survival alone, even if we do nothing but sleep and rest, demands that our energies be replenished. That is an indication of how importantly we should take our activities, in order that they truly deserve to be supplied thus. Ought we to support with food an uncontrolled, self-indulgent life?

Vice-versa, we ought to take our diet seriously because all our activities depend upon it. Eating is so essential, that we should do it in full awareness, not on the side and together with other activities. To combine eating and work is preposterous. The 'working lunch' is a monstrosity. To eat while standing or walking around shows a lack of respect for our food. When we combine eating with watching TV, with a loud and vehement discussion, with a demanding book, or with any other activity that we carry on in order to save time, then we do not do justice to our food and give it the attention it deserves. To eat with awareness does not only mean to eat healthily, but also to lend a deliberate dignity to the act of eating. We can attain that when we eat with the thought that this food sustains and prolongs our life. We feel how precious life is to us. Food should be just as precious.

We should be engaged enough in the act of eating to be grateful even for simple foods—a piece of bread, an apple, a baked potato—and feel them to be filled with life. Refined and luxurious meals are wonderful: they are an exuberant celebration of thanks to the earth and to god, the creator. But our contentment should not depend on having such meals.

In India, the Goddess Annapurna gives rice, the basic foodstuff, to the people every year through the riches of the harvest. *Anna* means rice, but its fundamental meaning is 'substance', 'material'. For food is the basic material of our body and of all bodies in creation. Food is, quite simply, creation. Those to whom creation is holy honour every sort of food, and eat it with gratitude and respect.

Sleeping

Who does not welcome sleep? Tired after a full day, anyone would look forward to sleeping—a period of time without awareness of time, without the consciousness of our waking hours, without the intrusion of outer sensations. Is it not strange that we long for this emptiness that sleep constitutes? Would it not be more natural to be afraid of this interruption of our stream of consciousness, of breaking the unity of our everyday world? Among those things that are repeated daily, sleep is the most mysterious. That after a day's varied activities, it is precisely the barest inactivity that attracts and refreshes us the most is something that should give us pause for thought.

The Romantics knew that sleepers are also weaving their threads in the tapestry of life. We seem to need the non-being of sleep as a way to offset or moderate powerful, often sharp and painful impressions on our senses and emotions. In sleep we process the day's multiplicity and immerse it in simplicity, subtly recasting our memories of it. When we wake up in the morning, we remember the previous day, but its experiences have lost their biting sharpness.

It is tiredness that necessitates sleep, giving us refreshment through non-being. Tiredness is the strict custodian of moderation. We can eat and drink in excess, argue loudly and roar with laughter, take drugs or dedicate ourselves to exercise. Only later do the consequences teach us that we have contravened the doctrine—'Moderation in all things'. But to stay awake excessively is not easy. Tiredness blunts our sensual experiences, and we perceive less and less. We must come to a stop at some point.

If we would only learn from sleep, and pause in the midst of daily plenitude to savour a few moments of stillness, through meditation, contemplation, unintentional simple being.

Sleep is sacred to us. We are ashamed to wake those who are sleeping, we do not like to look them in the face. We feel timidity when confronted with the uncanny mystery of sleep. It is the daily executor of the golden mean, in small things as in large.

Dreams can make us happy or disturb us—they are unreliable and sometimes vexatious. But sleep gives us a foretaste of celestial bliss.

Bathing

There are activities which should never be hurried or cut short. When parents say to their children, 'Tonight you must sleep early, so that you feel rested tomorrow,' they are joking. Sleep takes as much time as it takes. It is the same with bathing. To be sure, we say, 'I'll just jump in the shower quickly,' but in reality that is as absurd as 'quickly' taking a bath. We have to undress and also get the water temperature right. Our body reacts to the water temperature. It should not be steaming hot, so that the heart is not strained by the adjustment; it should be neither too hot nor too cold. But the temperature of the water should differ somewhat from that of our body, so that we are cooled down or warmed up.

In Indian villages, a modern shower would not satisfy people. They want to dip their whole body in the water. They look for a pool or a river and let themselves be enveloped completely in the watery element, dunking their heads two or three times under the surface before they climb out.

When totally enveloped by water the body feels heavy, for it can only be moved slowly. Strange that this heaviness nevertheless feels like floating, being lifted, carried along protected by the water. This pleasant feeling of being suspended in the water removes the sense of threat one might feel when immersed up to one's neck. We feel one with it, this fluid element. The sense of floating, drifting, being fluid rises in our minds, and much that has pressed on us, burdened us or stirred us up falls away.

If we are aware that water is a purifying element, that gently does its work through contact with our body, then we can yield to it even more easily. Abandonment is the appropriate response to water. It thanks us it by enveloping our bodies and washing every pore.

When we step out, dry ourselves off and put our clothes back on, we feel a freshness on our skin that takes us by surprise everytime—and spurs us on to bolder actions than we were capable of before the bath.

VII Singing

What we find difficult to express in conversation may be easier to express in song. When we sing, we are not bothered by feelings of shame or embarrassment. When we sing, we know neither fear nor frustration. We even curb our feelings of anger or of adoration when we sing. In conversation these extreme effects can surge up unpredictably, can agitate us or overpower us. In singing we are slower, we move within the melody and seek in it an expression for our feelings.

Not that we should, once embroiled in some heavy or awkward dialogue, suddenly break out in song. But whenever we are at a loss, whenever we are hard-pressed, we can take a step back, and sing. In the evening, when the day's events press too hard on us—sing! In the morning, when it seems hard to find a beginning—sing! We invent the text and the melody ourselves, and guide our voice in such a way as given expression to our emotions.

The text says in simple words what moves us. In songs we articulate our troubles, our frustration or perplexity, our fear or uncertainty. As we sing these tensions gradually resolve themselves. Our moods are superseded by a more general, a more basic feeling: 'Such is life.' A consciousness that all our inner turbulence is only temporary, that it will clear away, and that—even when it imposes itself strongly on us—we need not, therefore, accept it. As we sing, we sense that the violence of our feelings is something petty and overstrained. As we sing, we open them up to a breadth of space and time—meaning also the space and time of the heart. Uptight and trivial emotions dissolve into sustaining, soul-spreading feelings.

Why do performances of opera move us so strongly? Is it not grotesque for people tossing everyday conversations? Certainly! But through song they elevate words into a sphere of symbolic meaning.

Why are choirs so popular among us? Precisely because they give us a voice, because singing together presents us with a profound sensation of life and community. It is emotional without being tempestuous; it is not egoistic, but calls for harmony and cheerful spirits.

Listening

Listening counts as a special human quality. Everyone respects people who listen well—everyone wants to be a good listener. The reverse is heeded less: Are my words to others worth being listened to? Or do I exploit their benevolence with my chatter about banal and vulgar subjects? And should I quietly put up with the thoughtless talk of others, or should I interrupt them with a rebuke or by withdrawing from the conversation—which would after all be more honest?

Listening well is not simply a matter of giving other people as much time to speak as one takes for oneself. Listening well really has nothing to do with a fair allocation of speaking and listening. Rather, it is a question of the intensity and sensibility of mutual attention. A composed and intelligent dialogue can occur when it is granted an undisturbed space in which ideas and experiences can be unfolded. That demands partners who respect one another. With listening goes a kind of speech that one is happy to listen to, that evokes appreciation which satisfies curiosity, that is appropriate to the other's horizon of understanding, and that for these reasons one will happily involve oneself in.

If one is unwilling as a speaker to open oneself up, then there is no need to expect a sympathetic listener. If one is not a sympathetic listener, one cannot expect the other to open up.

The gift of listening is a blessing. It demands a calm willingness to involve oneself in the situation of the other. By using the resources of our own experience, empathetic imagination and intellect, we attempt to listen deeper and more carefully to the other. For the meantime, our own rational or emotional impulses must defer to them. How deeply we have understood the other is shown in the questions which we put to the person speaking. Appropriate questions as such drive the conversation forward, deepen it, and guide it out of self-absorption towards broader horizons. These questions inspire trust and self-knowledge. They hold up—the more selflessly, the more clearly—a mirror to the other's face.

The most successful, and delightful, conversations are those between two good listeners.

Loving

The thing which gives us greatest joy and which from time to time we long for, physical love, is possible without effort, scene-setting or preparation. To take delight in it, by contrast we leave everything behind, lay aside all aids, strip off all embellishments, abandon our usual consumer attitudes that artificially pacify us with TV, music and hasty ready-prepared meals—all of that goes, and we are transformed back into poor, naked beings, so that two bodies can encounter and touch one another, without aid or artifice. Even though there exists a gigantic erotic industry offering us all sorts of devices, perfumes, pills, lingerie, and seductive music—in the end we are thrown back on ourselves: on the encounter of two bodies.

It is true that our feelings and thoughts support our bodies, so that this encounter can be a success. We attempt to recognise, by imagination and intuition, the other person's needs, and to satisfy them. And yet it remains in the end the work of our physical bodies through which we find the coveted happiness, the longed-for ecstasy of this moment.

In this divestment lies the challenge of physical love. When one is naked one cannot hide one's weaknesses and blemishes. When one is naked only the elemental human attributes count, not prestige or learning, and nothing borrowed or pretended.

As much as we are reliant on our bodies, still they only unite with each other to a very small extent. They are never dissolved or melted into each other; they remain two solid, separate bodies. The unification consists in an intense consciousness, an ecstatic feeling that rises to a climax and then leaves us. The tragic aspect of physical love is this imperfection.

For that reason, the religious mystics turned away from their body, and sought a unification that makes two people wholly and forever one. Was their quest successful? Is their unification with the divine man not also an ecstatic feeling which passes? Does any perfect unification exist? This unification with the divine also needs a total divestment—that is clear; and not just of one's clothes, but of habits, attachments and aversions, futile thoughts and feeling. This self-exposure goes further than exposing one's body. Perhaps, the, the unification that results is less imperfect?

Grieving

A death, an accident, a severe disappointment, or a failure tears apart the fabric of our life. What was normal and self-evident before is suddenly askew, wrong, distorted. Nothing fits together any longer. Our home and those dearest to us appear strange and foreign. We were so happy with our circumstances—and now this!

We begin to grieve for a past reality. Our memory throws itself upon it with all its force. We idealise what no longer exists: those now dead, spent health, lost happiness, places we lived in long ago. Everything good and valuable can all of a sudden only be found in the past, and the present is filled with enraged grief. Any idea of a future to strive for is screened off from us.

How unjust we are towards life! One of the important exercises which we should begin to practice as early as possible in life is to accept that every day brings changes. If one grasps that fully, one will never expect that any condition—be it health or illness, happiness or disappointment, success or failure—is lasting. Such practice aims for an inner awareness and detachment that reckons with everything, and presupposes nothing. If we live in this state of readied awareness, we feel gratitude for every moment of happiness, and with an intensity that we had not suspected previously.

We feel grief at every loss, yet without being overpowered by it. We do not suppress our grief. But this is not the destructive, corrosive grief that will sacrifice everything on account of one loss. Grief should help us to say goodbye with dignity. It is the positive answer to changes in our life. Grieving is a power that can heal the wound, the fissure that loss has torn through us. It cannot make us forget what has happened—on the contrary, through it, our memory of past happiness or lost love can be nurtured. Grief reconciles us with loss by putting what once was in a perspective that includes our whole life, even the whole of creation. Then we participate once more, and in a new and unsuspected way, in life's fullness.

Grieving needs one thing, however: Time. Only when we give ourselves plenty of time to grieve will its healing forces develop; just as a wound only heals when nature is left to take charge of our body.

Writing letters

In the writing of a letter, a person's creative will and their urge to import information are united in the task of shaping a text for a single person, the letter's recipient. By virtue of its form, which required effort, talent and time to attain, a letter presents the recipient with something very personal.

To write a letter, it takes perhaps one or two hours. The writer chooses his words: they should be moulded into a pleasing and significant form. But the recipient may take only a couple of minutes to read it. The personal aspect lies precisely in this difference. The real currency of our age is time. Whoever invests that much time and effort in order to communicate something to only one person must be very attached to that person. Someone writing a letter manifests three sorts of attachment, in fact: to the addressee, to an appropriate form of words, and to true communication.

This noble activity, letter-writing, has become old-fashioned. Today emails are written at speed, answered at speed—one click and they are erased again. An email exchange is almost like a conversation conducted in writing. It has all of the provisional, imperfect, approximate qualities that we are familiar with in conversation. A letter, in contrast, not only requires a long time to write, it may be several days until it arrives and is read. And many more days will pass until a reply is written, sent, and reaches the first correspondent. During this time both must wait. Each waits with those strange and precious sensations of anticipation, concern and apprehension: how was the letter or its reply received? Does the recipient react with the sense of relief intended, with the hoped-for feelings of joy? Does he honour the care and attention paid out in time's own currency? This slowly alternating rhythm between two people is destroyed when letters are replaced by immediate communication.

In India, politeness and respect demand that one communicates with older, respected people by means of handwritten letters. The personality of the writer is revealed in a much subtler form through handwriting. It makes the letter unique. Handwriting and content together lend it an unmatchable dignity. Such letters lose much of their character and import when they are reproduced in books, for instance. But collected in a folder, such letters are documents of a life, of a relationship—even later, when the correspondents are no longer with us.

Giving presents

When my mother was given a present, for a few moments she would be overjoyed and very grateful; but then she would become pensive and even worried. 'How can I pay them back?' she asked herself. At once she planned to give a present in return. It was almost unbearable for her to receive a present without responding with an equally, or even more expensive gift. Otherwise she would feel indebted to the giver, and her world would not be in balance.

In this attitude—is it not typical for us Europeans—the material value and the effort expended in finding or making the present are what we take into consideration. That is how much the present is worth. We appraise the level of estimation and respect in which we are held by the giver accordingly. This makes matters clear and takes the burden off our shoulders. But does this way of responding to presents really do justice to the present and the person who gave it?

Giving a present is a way to express a positive attitude towards the recipient. It signals values such as friendship, love, thanks and recognition. A carefully selected present says a great deal about how the present-giver evaluates us. Seen in this way, the gift is a mirror held up to the person to whom it is given.

The act of giving does not try to attain anything; it is not calculated to produce a certain response. To think of 'paying back' the giver immediately shows a lack of respect for the generosity with which the present was given us. It is as if we were to give the present straight back to the giver.

Someone giving a present is revealing themselves, and thus making themselves vulnerable. If we do not know how to receive a gift in the same spirit as it was given, we go against the intrinsic affirmation of the act of giving. Real giving is thus only fulfilled through the proper acceptance of the gift.

Proper acceptance entails in the first place an attitude of thanks, of pleasure, of liberality. We want to receive with the same breadth of spirit with which the gift was given. The giving of presents occurs in a space of inner freedom, in which two people feel drawn to one another, discover one another and manifest what they have in common through the act of giving. We can only give to people like ourselves.

Telephoning

With a book in my hand I sit in my apartment on the Middle Rhine and read a short story about an Indian village. The telephone rings—it is an acquaintance from New York. I am suddenly present on three continents at once. When absorbed in writing I am startled by the sound of the telephone, however soft it may be. When I answer, questioningly, 'Hello?' for a few seconds I do not register who is there at the other end of the line, even after I have heard their name. The human voice, so close to my ear, recoils off the surface of my inner world.

Is it mentally healthy to leap across countries and continents like this, to carry on conversations with people who live in different situations, whose freedoms and constraints, problems and tensions, whose joy and sadness have such different sources? Can we understand each other?

The simultaneity of a telephone conversation is constructed purely through the voice, whose tone may even be distorted and unclear. Facial expressions and body language, which reveal so much, are hidden. If they could be seen then we could interpret words and tones of voice more precisely. If we know too little about the other, then we cannot express on the telephone all the impulses or ask all the questions we might like.

Our imagination demands to see the body, the physical movements that attach to the voice. And so a voice on the telephone involuntarily suggests to me a person's appearance—although when I meet the unknown person later, I am often astonished how wide off the mark my imagined picture of them was. Thus we should beware of confiding much over the telephone to a person we have never seen. To get to know them, we need their body, their gaze, their gestures.

And yet, for all that, what a gift of technology! The indistinct tone of a voice is often enough to spontaneously reawaken an old intimacy. Then the exchange of information takes second place to the resonance of the voice and the individuality of its speech. That well-known sound enthuses us, renews friendships, awakens memories: that way of laughing, that faint clearing of the throat, the pause at certain junctures in the conversation—an acoustically measurable, precise frequency of the voice carries the mysteries of a life and a relationship over thousands of kilometers to our ear.

VIII Seeking

We are seeking when we have an idea of what we hope to find. We have lost or misplaced something; perhaps we are seeking a word that has not occurred to us, or a name. In a shop we seek out a pair of trousers that fits us, or a pretty summer dress. Every day we seek things, we are constantly in search of something. Our thoughts and expectations are directed in front like sprinters, their upper bodies bent forward, racing and racing. If they stopped they would fall over! We seek people—nice colleagues, helpful bosses, friends, people with whom we can chat, ramble, argue, or go to the theatre. We seek places where we feel at ease, and times in which we can relax. We seek ideas, plans, fantasies, stories. We are always seeking, we cannot stop. The very multiplicity of our searches ceases to be concrete, and we no longer have any internal image of what we seek. We search without knowing what for. We search further in the mechanical belief that when we have found 'it', we will know—this is it! This belief drives us on.

But we never reach the point we have long been striving for, at which we can say—this is it! Our notions of what we really want, as unclear as they were to begin with, gain nothing in clarity by the many goals which we have already succeeded in reaching. Our life never fulfils itself, because we invent new expectations, and carry on with the race. It is part of our being, always to want more, to live our life better than before. We never believe that we already hold the whole of our life in our hands.

Like a flower, which, as long as it lives, strives towards the light, like the roots of a tree, which, as long as they are alive, seek water, we too seek to fulfill our lives on an ever larger scale. That impoverishes us.

It is good to strive for ever deeper fulfillment. But it is better to pause, to sit up, look around and within ourselves, and say—this is it! What I have achieved, what I am—that is fulfillment, in this moment. It is better to say—I have found, and found anew. It is better to celebrate what we have found and that we have found it. And to know—when I need seek no further, then comes the greatest fulfillment.

Thanking

Requests and expressions of gratitude are such common acts that they do not seem worthy of contemplation. From childhood on, we were taught to be polite and say 'Please' and 'Thank you'. They were and still are seen as magic words that open the doors to polite society. And yet it often seems as if 'Thank you' means no more than 'Stop! That's enough!' Or thanking may be merely an opportunity to hint that one is about to ask for something else.

Yet thanking signifies in the first place a confident, positive 'Yes' to a particular person and whatever we may have received from them. Taken more generally and symbolically, thanking is the affirmation and recognition of the existence of those that have given to us, and of the things that were given. In an even broader sense, thanking is the affirmation of creation, both animate and inanimate: A feeling of gratitude for being itself.

We accept both giver and gift into the circle of our life, allow them to be near us at least for a certain period, and perhaps even let them into the more intimate regions of our tastes, habits and feelings. In this way, thanking becomes a challenge to our will and ability to do justice to the new. That entails both respecting the giver's intentions and learning discretion in our own gift-giving.

Thanking brings obligations just as a request does, and thanks should not therefore be given too casually. Through the expression of thanks we lift what is material onto a spiritual level. The giver's thoughts are in the material gift—often secret, often unconscious thoughts. The gift is to us something like a riddle: what does it express? The kind of gratitude we express in return depends on our answer—or our failure to find any answer. The thoughts of the giver envelop the gift like a mist or a blinding light, extending out towards us.

We must, then, keep the presence of mind and power to reject the gift, if that is necessary, in order not to be obliged to thank the giver for it. To thank an unpleasant person weakens us. For a disproportionately generous gift we will only be able to give shame-faced thanks.

When the opportunistic motive is clear, accepting and thanking for a gift is already halfway to acquiescence in the dealing that will follow. To thank in such cases would rob us of our freedom.

Parting

Every time we suddenly stop seeing people with whom we have been together for many days, it affects us deeply. Parting is death in miniature, it is said. Does parting then signify a transition from being to non-being? But it is only the senses that are no longer party to the presence of the beloved. We no longer see and hear him, can no longer hold out our hand to him. Why does it comfort us so little to know that the departed is really 'still there'—just not before our eyes?

Time itself protests against our desire to be always with our beloved. The essence of time is change: it rules over the arrival, presence, and departure of others. The Buddha was aware that change is the unstable basis of life, and that it is just this which causes suffering. He meditated on the overcoming of suffering, by means of the overcoming of time. How might that be possible?

It is possible if we accept our sensory perception, which presents us with a current of time, filled with unceasing change, as only one mode of experience. The second level is an atemporal, unchanging present. Merely to contemplate this as a possibility can daunt us. In reality, however, it is comforting, relieving, blissful. We come closest to it in sleep, in prayer and meditation, in unoccupied or happy moments, and in moments of deep concentration or effort. Then the feeling of time's passing retracts, shrinks into a single point; then we have a profound intimation of what awaits us after death. Then we experience a slipping out of time as the quenching of our desires.

Such an experience is open to all of us; we must simply be able to accept it without fear. The result of such presentiments is that the heavy hand of the past, and of the future too, is lifted from us. The past no longer oppresses us with its mistakes, sins, missed opportunities and unfulfilled wishes. Our fear of the future becomes weaker. It becomes clear that past and future are mysteriously but really present to us in this very moment. The sensual and painful forces of our psyche, their attraction and repulsion gradually lessen. Equilibrium arises. Like all valuable acquisitions it needs practice. We will not be spared joy and pain, but they will not overpower us any longer. Parting remains parting, but we experience each farewell as a link in a long chain, in which parting and reunion are bound together. It is this bond which gives the chain its strength.

Arriving

One can only arrive if one has departed. The pressure and expectation which surround one's setting-off can only be absorbed when one arrives.

The mystery of arrival is that everything is new, or appears new. On the one hand that can be frustrating: all the familiar maneuvers and little habits, which make our everyday lives pleasant because we do not have to decide consciously to follow each of them, become inoperative after our arrival. Where do we put the house keys? How do we get our daily paper in the morning? Where can we read and write our emails? These and dozens of other things must be thought of, fixed, and made into a routine. When we return to our previous environment we must remember: Where are the light switches? When does the postman come? It costs energy, monopolises our attention: first of all we have to compose a new daily routine for ourselves.

On the other hand, the new is an opportunity. When we arrive, we are often so overpowered by joy and expectation that this already suspends our sense of the everyday. We meet friends again. We experience unfamiliar landscapes and things we have longed for. Then arrival is the exhilarating counterpart of everyday life, and we are more than willing to renounce our daily rituals. The excitement of the new makes arriving feel like a new birth.

That is precisely the point of arriving: to interpret our life anew. The challenge consists not only in relearning all our little everyday maneuvers, but also in thinking over the fundamental decisions of our lives. Arriving grants us a certain freedom, in that nothing is yet fixed. We can choose. We can engage anew with people, facts, values, or we can turn away from them. We experience them almost as we did at our first encounter with them, and have the chance to test our reflexes and assessments of value. Are they just? Do they still fit with our hopes and ideals?

If we extend this period of arrival for as long as possible, then we can maintain this freshness of perception, we can live creatively. That is demanding, for the momentum of joy and expectation may not always carry us. Yet this drawn-out arrival is more intense and more worth living than the patterns of an everyday life on which we no longer reflect.

Afterword

This slender book of poetic reflections was conceived in February 2008 when a German friend and I wandered around the ancient city of Rome. It was my first visit, and I was overwhelmed by the strong presences radiated by the historical buildings, avenues, squares, fountains, steps, and cemeteries. It seemed to me that with every step we entered a new field of emanations, some sacred, some related to every-day life. It was then that I realised how we in fact move within ever-changing domains of symbolic meaning, projected by nature, by historicity, by the tools of daily life, by the persons and objects we are surrounded with.

Would it not be appropriate to record the experience how we are able to enter into such a life filled with symbolic meaning by consciously considering our surroundings and becoming aware of how we act and react in them? While still in Rome, I wrote the chapter which is titled 'Climbing steps'. In the next few months I jotted down text after text wherever I was, in Germany and in India, in trains and on planes, then wrote and rewrote them on my computer. It was an intense, often trance-like experience.

It became the sum total of the experience I had among the people of India, in her villages and suburbs. When I arrived in India forty years ago, I felt inspired by the day-to-day life of farmers, artisans and workmen who extract a quantum of joy and meaning from life by throwing it open to the cosmic realities—to the daily cycle of the sun, the cycle of the moon from full moon to new moon, to the significances of the earth and the rivers, the trees and the clouds. I tried to understand the ordinary activities of life like sleeping and bathing, breathing and sitting which are given so much weight among the 'simple'. Then there were the interpersonal activities like asking questions, greeting, loving, writing letters which emerge with fresh meaning once the basic significances of life within nature and cosmos are being comprehended.

More and more I also realised that my study of Sri Ramakrishna's conversations with his disciples and my translation of Rabindranath Tagore's poems from Bengali to German have also suffused these reflections.

I have been at pains to steer clear of theological statements. True, I have learnt immensely from the study of Hinduism as well as from the fellowship with many Hindus; the realisations of my life as a Catholic, too, ring through this book. But my texts are not meant to inform my readers of any particular religion; they do not edify or teach piety. Rather, they modestly wish to share what I have discerned, bestowing to all the importance due within the Great Scheme of Things.

This scheme is symbolised by the eight chapters of the book; they signify a process: In the morning (I) a fresh beginning is attempted; we venture out into daily life (II), and mingle among people (III). We reflect about our everyday activities while we are engaged in them (IV); this makes us stop and pause (V), ready to refresh our mental and emotional energies (VI). Thereafter we are prepared for new and more mature encounters (VII) and finally for the liberating views of a fulfilled human being (VIII).

I thank my friend Matthew Pritchard who, on a visit to Santiniketan, spontaneously translated the German original. Thank you, Nirmalkanti Bhattacharya, for bringing the book to the notice of the publisher. Many thanks to Niyogi Books, especially to Jyoti Kumari, for publishing the manuscript with efficiency and aesthetic care.

Martin Kämpchen

Santiniketan, September 2012

